POCKET
PRAYERS
FOR PILGRIMS

Other books in the series:

Pocket Prayers for Troubled Times
Compiled by John Pritchard

Pocket Celtic Prayers
Compiled by Martin Wallace

Pocket Graces
Compiled by Pam Robertson

Pocket Prayers for Children
Compiled by Christopher Herbert

Pocket Prayers: The Classic Edition
Compiled by Christopher Herbert

Pocket Prayers for Advent and Christmas
Compiled by Jan McFarlane

Pocket Prayers for Commuters
Compiled by Christopher Herbert

Pocket Prayers for Healing and Wholeness
Compiled by Trevor Lloyd

Pocket Prayers for Marriage
Compiled by Andrew and Pippa Body

Pocket Words of Comfort
Compiled by Christopher Herbert

POCKET PRAYERS
FOR PILGRIMS

COMPILED BY
JOHN PRITCHARD

CHURCH HOUSE
PUBLISHING

Church House Publishing
Church House
Great Smith Street
London SW1P 3AZ

ISBN 978 0 7151 4238 7

Published 2011 by Church House Publishing

Emails: copyright@churchofengland.org

Designed by www.penguinboy.net
Printed and bound by Ashford Colour Press Ltd, Hants

CONTENTS

INTRODUCTION

'Now is the time to go on pilgrimage.' So said Chaucer in his Canterbury Tales, and now does indeed seem to be the time when many people are going on pilgrimage. Record numbers of people are travelling to Jerusalem, Rome and Santiago de Compostela. Cathedrals report burgeoning visitor numbers. Eighty-six percent of the British population go into a church for some reason or other during the year.

There is something quite fundamental to human well-being about travelling somewhere together. People do it for many different reasons, but usually physical exercise combines with personal, intellectual and spiritual refreshment. There is a communal dimension as well as the opportunity to ponder alone.

For Christians and other believers pilgrimage is a time to be with God in order to be more fully in life. It reflects in miniature the journey we take with God from birth to death, and then on to the heavenly city. Pilgrimage is therefore an inward journey as well as an outward one. Because it's different from normal life pilgrimage puts us somewhat off-balance, and therefore, perhaps, we are more open to God.

The purpose of this small book is to put into the hands of today's pilgrims some prayers and reflections to make the journey more rewarding. They can be used at the beginning, middle and end of each day or at the beginning, middle and end of the whole pilgrimage, always remembering that our entire life is actually a pilgrimage with and towards God.

May these prayers enrich the journey.

+John Pritchard
Bishop of Oxford

TO BE A PILGRIM

The idea of pilgrimage has a certain romance, but it actually emerges from a robust and demanding source – the intentional, and often challenging, journeys made by people of faith to significant places. Pilgrim, beware! The habit of pilgrimage has been well known for as long as faithful people have looked for a deeper encounter with God, whether travelling to the Promised Land, to Jerusalem, to the places of medieval pilgrimage or to a nearby cathedral in the present day. There is a deep and liberating compulsion in huge numbers of people 'to be a pilgrim'.

I was glad when they said to me,
'Let us go to the house of the Lord!'
Our feet are standing, within your gates, O Jerusalem.
Jerusalem – built as a city
that is bound firmly together.
To it the tribes go up, the tribes of the Lord,
as was decreed for Israel,
to give thanks to the name of the Lord.
For there the thrones for judgement were set up,
the thrones of the house of David.
Pray for the peace of Jerusalem:
'May they prosper who love you.
Peace be within your walls,
and security within your towers.'
For the sake of my relatives and friends
I will say, 'Peace be within you.'
For the sake of the house of the Lord our God,
I will seek your good.

Psalm 122

Then [Jesus] took the twelve aside and said to them,
'See, we are going up to Jerusalem.'

Luke 18.31

Now on that same day two of them were going to a
village called Emmaus, about seven miles from
Jerusalem, and talking with each other about all these
things that had happened. While they were talking
and discussing, Jesus himself came near and went with
them.

Luke 24.13–15

May the God who called our father Abraham
to journey into the unknown,
and guarded him and blessed him,
protect me too and bless my journey.
May his confidence support me as I set out,
may his Spirit be with me on the way,
and may he lead me back to my home in peace.
Those I love I commend to his care.
He is with them, I shall not fear.
As for myself,
may his presence be my companion,
so that blessing may come to me
and to everyone I meet.
Blessed are you, Lord,
whose presence travels with his people.

Jewish Prayer Book

Who would true valour see,
let him come hither;
one here will constant be,
come wind, come weather;
there's no discouragement
shall make him once relent
his first avowed intent
to be a pilgrim.

Whoso beset him round
with dismal stories,
do but themselves confound;
his strength the more is.
No lion can him fright;
he'll with a lion fight,
but he will have the right
to be a pilgrim.

No goblin nor foul fiend
can daunt his spirit;
he knows he at the end
shall life inherit.
Then, fancies fly away;
he'll not fear what men say;
he'll labour night and day
to be a pilgrim.

John Bunyan, 1628–8

Pilgrim God,
you are our origin and destination.
Travel with us, we pray, in every pilgrimage of faith,
and every journey of the heart.
Give us the courage to set off,
the nourishment we need to travel well,
and the welcome we long for at journey's end.
So may we grow in grace and love of you
and in the service of others,
through Jesus Christ our Lord.

May God,
who has received you by baptism into his Church,
Pour upon you the riches of his grace,
That within the company of Christ's pilgrim people
You may daily be renewed by his anointing Spirit,
And come to the inheritance of the saints in glory.

Common Worship

LIFE AS A PILGRIM

One of the most easily recognized metaphors for life is that it is a journey or pilgrimage full of incident, joys and crises, periods when we are toiling uphill and times when the sun is always shining on our back. Life is a journey with God, with ourselves and with others – a community of pilgrims, learning as we go. Viewed as a pilgrimage, life clearly requires of us the same qualities of courage, determination, flexibility, resilience and hope that we see in the focused, time-limited pilgrimages we undertake in our holidays. In both cases the most important gift to hold on to is the promise of God to be our guardian and our guide.

Some people travel in straight lines,
sitting in metal boxes, eyes ahead,
always mindful of the target,
moving in obedience to coloured lines and white lines.

Some people travel round in circles,
trudging in drudgery, eyes looking down,
knowing only too well their daily, unchanging round,
moving in response to clock and habit,
journey never finished yet never begun.

I want to travel in patterns of God's making:
walking in wonder, gazing all around,
knowing my destiny, though not my destination,
moving to the rhythm of the surging of the Spirit,
a journey which, when life ends,
in Christ has just begun.

Adapted from Sunday Worship on BBC Radio 4

Let us make our way together, Lord; wherever you go
I must go: and through whatever you pass, there too
I will pass.

Teresa of Avila, 1515–82

Give me my scallop-shell* of quiet,
my staff of faith to walk upon,
my scrip of joy, immortal diet,
my bottle of salvation,
my gown of glory, hope's true gage;
and thus I'll take my pilgrimage

Sir Walter Raleigh, 1552–1618

A scallop shell was the token and sign that someone had made the pilgrimage to Santiago de Compostela.

My Lord God, I have no idea where I am going. I do not see the road ahead of me. I cannot know for certain where it will end. Nor do I really know myself, and the fact that I think I am following your will does not mean that I am actually doing so. But I believe the desire to please you does in fact please you, and I hope I have that desire in all that I am doing. I hope that I never do anything apart from that desire. And I know that if I do this you will lead me by the right road though I may know nothing about it. Therefore I will trust you always. Though I may seem to be lost and in the shadow of death I will not fear, for you are ever with me and you will never leave me to face my peril alone.

Thomas Merton, 1915-68

O Lord Jesus Christ, who hast said that thou art the way, the truth and the life; suffer us not at any time to stray from thee, who art the way; nor to distrust thy promises, who art the truth; nor to rest in any other thing, who art the life; beyond which there is nothing to be desired, neither in heaven, nor in earth.

Christian Prayers, 1578

Today we are far from home
and have lost the key to the door.
But you call us to go in
and find ourselves again.
Your invitation is to the interior life.
Your experience is that of persons
who regain a sense of themselves.
Benedict, teach us the way back to the heart,
in Christ our Lord.

Prayer on the shrine of St. Benedict at Fleury,

St-Benoit-sur-Loire

Teach us, O God,
to view our life here on earth
as a pilgrim's path to heaven,
and give us grace to tread it courageously
in the company of your faithful people.
Help us to set our affections on things above,
not on the passing vanities of this world,
and grant that as we journey on
in the way of holiness
we may bear a good witness to our Lord,
and serve all who need our help along the way,
for the glory of your name.

Hereford Cathedral

God the Sender, send us.
God the Sent, come with us.
God the Strengthener of those who go, empower us,
that we may go forever and wherever with you
Father, Son and Holy Spirit.

Anon.

Pilgrim God, there is an exodus going on in my life: desert stretches, a vast land of questions. Inside my head your promises tumble and turn. No pillar of cloud by day or fire by night that I can see. My heart hurts at leaving loved ones and so much of the security I have known. I try to give in to the stretching and the pain. It is hard, God, and I want to be settled, secure, safe and sure. And here I am feeling so full of pilgrim's fear and anxiety. O God of the journey, lift me up, press me against your cheek. Let your great love hold me and create a deep trust in me. Then set me down, God of the journey; take my hand in yours, and guide me ever so gently across the new territory of my life.

Joyce Rupp

God of glory,
the end of our searching,
help us to lay aside
all that prevents us from seeking your kingdom,
and to give all that we have
to gain the pearl beyond all price,
through our Saviour Jesus Christ.

Common Worship, Additional Collects

SETTING OUT

The most vulnerable time on a pilgrimage is when we are setting out. We don't know how difficult it will be or how well we will respond to its opportunities and stand up to its rigours. We may feel a real need for blessing, putting ourselves under the protection and guiding hand of God. It's also the time of greatest energy and hope with the prospect of discoveries, meetings and adventures yet unknown. We gain much if we can recover a sense of the Christian life as an adventure, rather than just a safe place.

Now the Lord said to Abram, 'Go from your country
and your kindred and your father's house to the land
that I will show you. I will make of you a great nation,
and I will bless you, and make your name great, so that
you will be a blessing. I will bless those who bless you,
and the one who curses you I will curse; and in you all
the families of the earth shall be blessed.
So Abram went, as the Lord had told him'.

Genesis 12. 1–4.

Lord God, Heavenly Father,
we thank you for protecting those who seek you
and for guiding those who hope for you.
We pray for your blessing
now as we enter our pilgrimage.
Save us from all evil, let no harm come upon us.
Protect our body and our soul.
Help us to be ready
for what you reveal to us on our way,
and when we reach our goal,
help us listen to your voice afresh
and be open to the renewal
of our life and our faith in you.

Anon.

A blessing on our departures,
without them we cannot walk the way.
A blessing on our companions,
bread of friendship, bread for the soul.
A blessing on all travellers
border-crossers, wanderers in strange lands.
A blessing on all the stages of the way
and those who give us guidance.
A blessing on all we leave behind
and on their journeys.
A blessing on our lostness and delays,
these too are life.
A blessing on our arrivals,
home-comings, new beginnings, bright horizons
A blessing on the Trinity of Journeys.
Giver of the Way, Jesus of the Way, Spirit of the Way.

Kathy Galloway, based on Psalm 139

Christ be with me, Christ within me
Christ behind me, Christ before me
Christ beside me, Christ to win me
Christ to comfort and restore me.

Christ beneath me, Christ above me
Christ in quiet, Christ in danger
Christ in hearts of those who love me
Christ in mouth of friend and stranger.

A version of St Patrick's Breastplate

Away O Soul, hoist instantly the anchor!
Cut the hawsers – haul out – shake out every sail!
Sail forth – steer for the deep waters only;
Reckless O Soul, exploring,
I with thee and thou with me,
for we are bound where mariner
has not yet dared to go,
and we will risk the ship, ourselves and all.
O my brave Soul.
O farther, farther sail!
O daring joy, but safe!
Are they not all the seas of God?
O farther, farther sail!

Walt Whitman, 1819–92

Companion of the Way,
you know the place where I have come from,
those I have loved and left.
You know those things
I have longed to bid farewell to.
Accompany my trembling feet
as I step onto a new road now.
Accompany my quivering hands
as they grapple with unfamiliar things.
Accompany my memory as I absorb new information.
Accompany my wandering legs
when I get lost and disorientated.
Accompany my heart
that I may be open to new possibilities of friendship.
Accompany me
when I tarnish the new place with my old mistakes.
Take my brave face in your hands
and my fears in your love.
Take the strain of being a beginner
and not yet competent.
Take the exhausting alertness of being unknown
and not yet loved
until I can return to those who love me
and tell them my story this day.
Accompany me as I enter this chapter on my own,
dear Companion of my way.

Tess Ward

May Almighty God
graciously direct you on your journey
and bring you in safety to the place
where you wish to go,
for his merciful love is known in all places
and he treats his family with tender kindness

May a band of angels go with you
and prepare the way before you:
may their comfort sustain you
and protect you from harm.

May Christ who is the Way, the Truth and the Life
be your companion;
may you follow the way of justice
and reach the reward of everlasting joy.
Anon.

May the strength of God pilot us,
may the power of God preserve us,
may the wisdom of God instruct us,
may the hand of God protect us,
may the way of God direct us,
may the shield of God defend us,
may the host of God guard us
against the snares of evil
and the temptations of the world.
St Patrick, 389–461

Set out!
You were born for the road.
You have a meeting to keep.
Where? With whom?
Perhaps with yourself.

Set out!
Alone or with others –
but get out of yourself.
You have created rivals;
you will find companions.
You envisaged enemies;
you will find brothers and sisters.

Set out!
Your head does not know
where your feet
are leading your heart.

Set out!
You were born for the road –
the pilgrim's road.
Someone is coming to meet you,
is seeking you
in the shrine at the end of the road,
in the shrine at the depths of your heart.

Go!
God already walks with you.
Anon.

SPECIAL PLACES

During the course of our pilgrimage, as well as at the end, we will probably come across special places that shiver with subdued holiness. These are places to pause and ponder, exploring the moment rather than constantly pressing on. These are 'thin' places where prayer has proved itself and the walls are soaked in the desires and praises of the people who have lingered there. As we experience this quality of 'otherness' in special places, we might then be reminded that, in fact, God awaits us at every moment and in every place.

God of special places,
thin with prayers and epiphanies,
meet us today and touch our lives,
that we may be reminded
in a world of change and anxiety
that only your presence is constant,
and only love is worthwhile.

Surely the Lord is in this place – and I did not know it!
How awesome is this place! This is none other than
the house of God, and this is the gate of heaven.
Genesis 28.16,17

Thank you, Father, for this ancient place of prayer:
for the faith that has blossomed here,
and for worship in all seasons offered here;
for lives that have been touched here,
and commitment stirred into life here.
As we tread in the footsteps
of our mothers and fathers in the faith
bless us and all who come here,
and speak to us with the whisper of your love,
for you are a God of renewal and of steadfastness,
now and forever.
Angela Ashwin

(On entering a church)
We adore you, Lord Jesus Christ, here and in all your churches throughout the world, and we bless you, because by your holy cross you have redeemed the world.

St Francis of Assisi, 1181–1226

Soul Places
where my soul is at home
and the longing in my soul
is echoed and met in the lonely place –
in the wild Highlands of my Scottish forebears
echoing down the centuries
to meet and touch the need I did not know I had.

Have you set these places, Lord?
Have you set these places
where our souls reach out of us
to something beyond?
Is it you calling us?
Does your soul yearn for us
as ours yearn for you?
Have you set places where our souls can touch –
yours and mine?

Others find these soul places in different ways.
Some find themselves meeting you
in ordered, tended gardens
or in the paths through soft woodlands
or in the gentle rolling hills and downs
or in the places set apart for seeking you
in buildings so soaked in prayer
that the very fabric breathes out
'Our Father' and 'Amen'.
Do you make these places, Lord
where my soul is at home with yours?

Beatrix Stewart (shortened)

Lord, you who called your servant Abraham
out of the town of Ur in Chaldea
and who watched over him during all his wanderings;
you who guided the Jewish people through the desert;
we pray for you to watch your servants who,
for the love of your name,
make a pilgrimage to [Santiago de Compostela].

Be for us,
a companion on our journey
a guide at our intersections
strength in our weariness
defence against dangers
shelter on the way
shade against the heat
light in the darkness
comfort in discouragement
and the power of our intention,

so that, under your guidance, safe and unhurt
we may reach the end of our journey,
and, strengthened with gratitude and power,
secure and filled with happiness,
we may return to our homes fulfilled,
through Jesus Christ, our Lord.

A version of the Roncesvalles blessing for pilgrims to Compostela

Visit this place, O Lord, we pray,
and drive far from it the snares of the enemy;
may your holy angels dwell with us
and guard us in peace,
and may your blessing be always upon us;
through Jesus Christ our Lord.
Common Worship Night Prayer

For a pilgrimage to the Holy Land
May the babe of Bethlehem be yours to tend;
the boy of Nazareth be yours for friend;
the man of Galilee his healing send;
the Christ of Calvary his courage lend;
the risen Lord his presence send;
and his holy angels defend you, to the end.
Ronald Brownrigg

THE JOURNEY

As we get under way on our pilgrimage – whether the pilgrimage of life or a special pilgrimage – we look to encounter God with new eyes and in new ways, in people we meet, places we stop, in nature's beauty and our own thoughts and feelings. God is never absent – our task is recognition. We need to put aside our normal habits of travel, which usually consist of getting from one place to another as quickly and comfortably as possible, and instead discover the riches of moving more slowly and looking more deeply. God's signature is all over his creation.

These twelve Jesus sent out with the following instructions:
'Take no gold, or silver, or copper in your belts, no bag for your journey, or two tunics, or sandals, or a staff; for labourers deserve their food. Whatever town or village you enter, find out who in it is worthy, and stay there until you leave. As you enter the house, greet it. If the house is worthy, let your peace come upon it; but if it is not worthy, let your peace return to you.'
Matthew 5a, 9-12

My journey is always just beginning,
a fresh new day,
On an old, old path.
That's the blessing,
that's where the hope blossoms.
However much I wandered yesterday
I can start again tomorrow,
And when all my tomorrows are used up,
I'll still have travelled.
It's the journey that counts,
not the arriving.
Mary Fleeson
© Mary Fleeson www.lindisfarne-scriptorium.co.uk

Lord, today brings
paths to discover
possibilities to choose
people to encounter
peace to possess
promises to fulfil
perplexities to ponder
power to strengthen
pointers to guide
pardon to accept
praises to sing
and a Presence to proclaim.
David Adam

Be thou a bright flame before me,
Be thou a guiding star above me,
Be thou a smooth path below me,
Be thou a kindly shepherd behind me,
Today, tonight and for ever.
St Columba, 521–97

Spirit of the wind, breathe down over these valleys,
Spirit of the air, breathe in our blood,
Spirit of the water, cleanse our eyes,
Spirit of the earth, warm our feet,
Spirit of fire, penetrate our hearts,
Spirit of fire, enter our minds,
Spirit of fire, strengthen our seeing,
that we may walk in truth on your living ground.
Jay Ramsay

God bless to you today
the earth beneath your feet,
the path on which you tread,
the work of your hand and mind,
the things which you desire.
And when the day is over,
God bless you to your rest.
Iona Community

We need to drink often when journeying, and that
may remind us of deeper truths.

Lord, our Living Water,
help me to remember you at all times of day.
Help me to realise
that you are essential to my existence;
that without you life is dry and filled with dust.
Help me to take the time to drink
at the spring of your refreshing and life-giving waters,
so that I in my turn
may live in a way that gives life to others.
Sally Welch

So, brethren, let us sing alleluia now, not in the
enjoyment of heavenly rest but to sweeten our toil.
Sing as travellers sing along the road, but keep on
walking. Sing, but keep on walking. What do I mean by
walking? I mean, press on from good to better. Paul
says there are some who go from bad to worse; but if
you press on, then you keep on walking. So sing
alleluia, and keep on walking.
St Augustine, 354–430

COMPANIONS ON THE WAY

The most exciting part of a pilgrimage is often the encounters we have on the way. God gives us such wonderful people to meet, from all backgrounds, coming on pilgrimage for all sorts of reasons. The key is to realise that we could be 'entertaining angels unawares' and so to treat everyone as a gift and a joy. There is a common language of pilgrimage, and variations on a common rhythm each day; it's the people we meet who enliven the day. When we get back it may well be that these conversations, with so many colourful characters, are the most vivid memories, reminding us of the continuing freshness of the characters in Chaucer's Canterbury Tales.

As they came near the village to which they were going, Jesus walked ahead as if he were going on. But they urged him strongly, saying, 'Stay with us, because it is almost evening and the day is now nearly over.' So he went in to stay with them. When he was at the table with them, he took bread, blessed and broke it, and gave it to them. Then their eyes were opened and they recognised him; and he vanished from their sight. They said to each other, 'Were not our hearts burning within us while he was talking to us on the road, while he was opening the scriptures to us?'

Luke 24.28–32 (NRSV)

Lord God,
whoever you bring into our path today,
may we see Christ in them,
and may they see Christ in us,
for your love's sake. Amen.

Here in the company of the neighbour
whom we know
and the stranger in the midst,
and the self from whom we turn,
we ask to love as Jesus loved.
Make this the time, good Lord,
when heaven and earth merge into one,
and we in word and flesh can grasp
that in Christ
there is neither Jew nor Gentile,
neither male nor female:
we are one in Jesus Christ
and for this we praise you.
Anon.

Let us remember those who have accompanied us at different times on our life journey:

- the light-filled ones, who enlivened our spirits with their teaching and the spark of their beliefs
- the risk takers, who faced their fears and took action, who sought justice even though they had to pay a price for it.
- the vulnerable ones, who allowed us to care for them, to be with them in their time of need.
- the faith-filled ones, who led us by their words and example, into deeper relationship with the Holy One.
- the brave ones, who walked through their struggles with hope, who taught us to trust through difficulties and sorrows.
- the nurturers, who sustained us physically or spiritually by their caring presence.
- the great lovers of life, whose humour and enthusiasm lifted our spirits and brought us joy.

Joyce Rupp (adapted)

Christ our companion,
you have given us friends to love us
and to be loved by us.
You have travelled with us
on our varied journeys.
You have encouraged and strengthened us
through the gift of one another
and the beauty of creation.
Continue to be our travelling companion
challenging us strongly,
 upholding us when we fall,
and nurturing us with your presence.

Elizabeth Baxter

Ruth said, 'Do not press me to leave you or to turn
back from following you. Where you go, I will go;
where you lodge, I will lodge; your people shall be my
people, and your God my God.'

Ruth 1.16

Pilgrim God, bless us with courage
where the way is fraught with dread or danger.
Bless us with graceful meetings
where the way is lonely.
Bless us with good companions
where the way demands a common cause.
Bless us with night vision where we travel in the dark,
keen hearing where we have not sight
to hear the reassuring sound of fellow travellers.
Bless us with good humour,
for we cannot travel lightly
weighed down with gravity.
Bless us with humility
to learn from those around us.
Bless us with decisiveness
when we have to move with speed.
Bless us with lazy moments
to stretch and rest and savour.
Bless us with love, given and received,
And bless us with your presence,
even when we know it in your absence.
Bless us, lead us, love us, and bring us home
bearing the gospel of life.
Kathy Galloway (adapted)

Through the night of doubt and sorrow
onward goes the pilgrim band,
singing songs of expectation,
marching to the promised land.
Clear before us through the darkness
gleams and burns the guiding light;
sister clasps the hand of brother
stepping fearless through the night.

One the light of God's own presence
o'er his ransomed people shed,
chasing far the gloom and terror,
brightening all the path we tread:
one the object of our journey,
one the faith which never tires,
one the earnest looking forward,
one the hope our God inspires.

Onward, therefore, fellow pilgrims
onward with the Cross our aid;
bear its shame, and fight its battle,
till we rest beneath its shade.
Soon shall come the great awakening,
soon the rending of the tomb;
then the scattering of all shadows,
and the end of toil and gloom.

B.S. Ingemann, 1789–1862

Christ our Guide,
stay with us on our pilgrimage through life:
when we falter, encourage us;
when we stumble, steady us;
and when we have fallen, pick us up.
Help us to become, step by step, more truly ourselves,
and remind us that you have travelled
this way before us.

Angela Ashwin

Then Peter and the other disciple set out and went
towards the tomb. The two were running together...

John 20. 3,4

ReSTING PLACeS

When we are on pilgrimage the times of rest and recovery are part of the joy, both during the day and when the day ends. During the day, we scan the path ahead; at night we review the day and learn its lessons. Again, the rhythm of movement and rest is part of the joy of travelling purposefully but without rushing. It's an example we would usually love to take back into the rest of our lives.

Good God,
this is tough.
My legs ache, my mouth is dry;
the path is always up, never down.
Can tomorrow be a rest day?
But who said the Christian way was easy?
Certainly not the young man on the cross.
Some of the journey of life is hard;
some is a plod;
and some is a dance.
Strengthen my resolve to seize the day
walk the extra mile
and receive your blessing,
which I ask in Jesus' name.

Gracious God
in you is our rest.
Thank you for the rhythms of the journey,
times of effort and times of relaxation,
times of encounter and times of solitude.
May our lives increasingly echo
the rhythms of your love
and the beauty of your presence
until the pilgrimage is complete
and we rest eternally in you.

Now that the sun has set,
I sit and rest, and think of you.
Give my weary body peace.
Let my legs and arms stop aching,
let my nose stop sneezing,
let my head stop thinking,
let me sleep in your arms.

African Dinka prayer

O Lord, you have searched me out and known me;
you know my sitting down and my rising up;
you discern my thoughts from afar.

You mark out my journeys and my resting place
and are acquainted with all my ways.

For there is not a word on my tongue,
but you, O Lord, know it altogether.

You encompass me behind and before
and lay your hand upon me.

Psalm 139. 1-4 (Common Worship Psalter)

Lord, it is night.

The night is for stillness
    Let us be still in the presence of God.

It is night after a long day.
    What has been done has been done;
    what has not been done has not been done;
    let it be.

The night is dark.
    Let our fears of the darkness
    of the world and of our own lives
    rest in you.

The night is quiet.
    Let the quietness of your peace enfold us,
    all dear to us,
    and all who have no peace.

The night heralds the dawn.
    Let us look expectantly to a new day,
    new joys,
    new possibilities.

In your name we pray.
Anon.

In peace I will lie down and sleep,
for it is you Lord, only, who make me dwell in safety.
Psalm 4.8

THROUGH MANY A DANGER

Pilgrimage would not be so exciting if there were no element of risk. There is always the possibility of losing our way or failing to find shelter, getting wet through or suffering painful blisters. These minor challenges can be timely reminders of the much larger risks taken by people throughout the world who are unwillingly on pilgrimage as refugees and exiles. Moreover, on our life pilgrimage no-one is exempt from suffering, and the price people pay can be very heavy. However, it's the unpredictability that makes life the adventure it is, and Christian pilgrims know they are called to support each other on the way. There's no guarantee of safety but there is the promise that, in Christ, we will not be overcome.

Pilgrim God,
our shoes are filled with stones,
our feet are blistered and bleeding,
our faces are stained with tears.
As we stumble and fall,
may we know your presence
in the bleeding and in the tears,
in the healing and the laughter
of our pilgrimage.

Kate McIhagga

Fix thou our steps, O Lord, that we stagger not at the
uneven motions of the world, but steadily go on to
our glorious home; neither censuring our journey by
the weather we meet with, nor turning out of the way
for anything that befalls us. The winds are often
rough, and our own weight presses us downwards.
Reach forth , O Lord, thy saving hand, and speedily
deliver us. Teach us, O Lord, to use this transitory life
as pilgrims returning to their beloved home; that we
may take what our journey requires, and not think of
settling in a foreign country.

John Wesley, 1703–91

Alone with none but thee, my God,
I journey on my way.
What need I fear, when thou are near
O king of night and day?
More safe am I within thy hand
than if a host did round me stand.

St Columba, c521–97

Lord God, we pray for all the bombed out,
burned out,
    driven out, relocated, wondering,
    wandering, sorrowing,
    unwilling pilgrims in this world.
Forgive us for our part in uprooting them,
restore their lives,
    assist your Church worldwide
    to be partners with them
    in the rebuilding of their lives.
We pray in the name of the Son of Man,
    who had no place to lay his head.

Arnold Kenseth and Richard Unsworth

As the rain hides the stars, as the autumn mist hides
the hills, as the clouds veil the blue of the sky, so the
dark happenings of my lot hide the shining of thy face
from me. Yet, if I may hold thy hand in the darkness, it
is enough. Since I know that, though I may stumble in
my going, thou dost not fall.

Celtic

God our deliverer,
as you led our ancestors through the wilderness,
so lead us through the wilderness of this world,
that we may be saved through Christ for ever.

Common Worship

God of our pilgrimage,
you sent your Son to our strange land
to bring us home to you;
give us your songs to sing,
that even in our exile
we may be filled with the breath of the Spirit
of Jesus Christ our Lord.

Common Worship

By the rivers of Babylon –
    there we sat down and there we wept.
    when we remembered Zion.
On the willows there
    we hung up our harps.
For there our captors
    asked us for songs,
and our tormentors asked for mirth, saying,
    'Sing us one of the songs of Zion!'
How could we sing the Lord's song
    in a foreign land?
If I forget you, O Jerusalem,
    let my right hand wither!
Let my tongue cling to the roof of my mouth,
    if I do not remember you,
    if I do not set Jerusalem
    above my highest joy.

Psalm 137. 1–6

The Lord is my pilot; I shall not drift, he lights me across the dark waters; he steers me in the deep channels: he keeps my log. He guides me by the star of his holiness for his name's sake. Though I sail amidst the hungers and tempests of life, I shall fear no danger, for you are near me; your love and care, they shelter me. You prepare a harbour before me in the homeland of eternity; you anoint the waves with oil; my ship rides calmly. Surely sunlight and starlight shall favour me in the voyage I take, and I shall rest in the port of my God for ever.

Anon. based on psalm 23

Guide me, O thou great Redeemer
pilgrim through this barren land.
I am weak, but thou are mighty;
hold me with thy powerful hand:
bread of heaven, bread of heaven,
feed me now and evermore.

Open now the crystal fountain,
whence the healing stream doth flow;
let the fiery cloudy pillar
lead me all my journey through:
strong deliverer, strong deliverer,
be thou still my strength and shield.

When I tread the verge of Jordan,
bid my anxious fears subside;
death of death, and hell's destruction,
land me safe on Canaan's side:
songs and praises, songs and praises
I will ever give to thee.

W. Williams 1717–91

ARRIVAL AND HOMECOMING

There are two moments of completion on a pilgrimage: one is arrival at the intended destination and the other is returning home and reflecting on the whole experience. Both these moments are deeply satisfying, although deep down we might recognize a new restlessness and a desire to return to the open road. Perhaps this echoes the Christian's eternal restlessness until we find our rest in God. Whether or not we go on pilgrimage again, the experience will have changed us.

51

Lord God, when you call your servants to endeavour
any great matter, grant us also to know that it is not
the beginning, but the continuing of the same, until it
be thoroughly finished, which yields the true glory;
through him who, for the finishing of your work, laid
down his life for us, our Redeemer, Jesus Christ.

Based on words of Sir Francis Drake, 1540–96

God of our pilgrimage
bring us with joy to the eternal city
founded on the rock,
and give to our earthly cities
the peace that comes from above;
through Jesus Christ our Lord.

Common Worship

All shall be Amen and Alleluia.
We shall rest and we shall see,
we shall see and we shall know,
we shall know and we shall love,
we shall love and we shall praise.
Behold our end which is no end.

St Augustine , 354–430

In gratitude, in deep gratitude
for this moment
   this experience
   these people,
we give ourselves to you.

Lead us out
to live as changed people
because we have shared the Living Bread
and cannot remain the same.

Ask much of us,
expect much from us,
enable much by us,
encourage many through us.

So, Lord, may we live to your glory,
both as citizens of earth
and citizens of the commonwealth of heaven
where our pilgrimage will be complete.

Anon.

Our journey is near its ending.
O great Giver of the Way,
where we have walked too roughly on the earth,
humble us.
Where we have missed a turning, redirect us.
Where we have failed to listen,
watch or wonder, wake our senses.
Where we have bypassed, backtracked,
or been dead to pain,
break our hearts and move us to compassion.

For you are not our small and sketchy map.
You are our ground, and you are holy.
You are the holy ground
of refugees and asylum seekers
of tramps and beggars
of street-sweepers and streetwalkers
of lonely hearts and long exiles
of small steps and great adventures.

Our journey's end is near.
But you and we go on together.
When we wake tomorrow, we shall still be with you.
Searching us out, gazing into our hearts,
watch, lest we follow paths that grieve you,
and lead us in the way that is everlasting.

Anon.

Bring us, O Lord God, at our last awakening, into the house and gate of heaven, to enter into that gate and dwell in that house, where there shall be no darkness nor dazzling, but one equal light; no noise nor silence, but one equal music; no fears nor hopes, but one equal possession; no ends nor beginnings, but one equal eternity; in the habitations of thy glory and dominion, world without end.

John Donne , 1571–1631

Support us, O Lord, all the day long of this troublesome life, till the shadows welcome, and the evening comes, the busy world is hushed, and the fever of life is over and our work is done. Then in thy mercy grant us a safe lodging, a holy rest and peace at the last.

The Book of Common Prayer (1928)

To finish the moment, to find the journey's end in every step of the road, to live the greatest number of good hours, is wisdom.

R.W. Emerson 1803–82

May the road rise up to meet you,
may the wind be always at your back,
may the sun shine upon your face,
the rains fall soft upon your fields
and, until we meet again.
may God hold you in the palm of his hand.
Celtic

How lovely is your dwelling place, O Lord of hosts!
My soul has a desire and longing to enter
the courts of the Lord;
my heart and my flesh rejoice in the living God.
The sparrow has found her a house
and the swallow a nest where she may lay her young;
at your altars, O Lord of hosts, my King and my God.
Psalm 84. 1–2 (Common Worship Psalter)

PILGRIMAGE AT HOME

Pilgrimage usually seems to be an exercise in exertion. It's about making a demanding physical journey of some sort. However, with a little imagination, we can make a pilgrimage in our own homes or local communities. All that is required is the will to travel in the mind and the heart. For further details see the Resources section. Praying around our home or community can be a liberating and stimulating experience, and give us a new appreciation of the spiritual resources we have all around us all the time. We can discover 'heaven in ordinary' and come alive to the presence of God who is both the origin and the goal of our earthly pilgrimage.

God bless this house from roof to floor,
God bless the windows and the door,
God bless us all evermore.
God bless the house with fire and light,
God bless each room with thy might,
God with thy hand hold us tight,
God be with us day and night.
David Adam (adapted)

O God, make the door of this house wide enough to
receive all who need human love and fellowship, and a
heavenly Father's care; and narrow enough to shut out
all envy, pride and hate. Make its threshold smooth
enough to be no stumbling block to children, nor to
straying feet, but rugged enough to turn back the
tempter's power: make it a gateway to thine eternal
kingdom.
Thomas Ken, 1637–1711

As soon as they left the synagogue, they entered the house of Simon and Andrew, with James and John. Now Simon's mother-in-law was in bed with a fever, and they told Jesus about her at once. He came and took her by the hand and lifted her up. Then the fever left her, and she began to serve them.

Mark 1.29–31

God of hearth and home,
bless this open door,
where Christ may enter by day and night;
bless this living room,
where friends may come as if by right;
bless this kitchen,
where love is found in form of food;
bless this bedroom, where failing energy is renewed.
bless this spare room, for healing and hope;
bless this bathroom, for cleansing and soap;
bless this garden where Creation is on view;
bless this home, that it may speak of You.

Circle us Lord;
keep protection near
and danger afar.

Circle us Lord;
keep hope within,
keep doubt without.

Circle us Lord;
keep light near,
and darkness afar.

Circle us Lord;
keep peace within,
keep evil out.
David Adam

May the peace of the Lord Christ go with you,
wherever he may send you.
May he guide you through the wilderness,
protect you through the storm.
May he bring you home rejoicing
at the wonders he has shown you.
May he bring you home rejoicing
once again into our doors.
Celtic Daily Prayer

SOME RESOURCES

- *Making a Pilgrimage*, Sally Welch (Lion 2009)
- *An Altar in the World*, Barbara Brown Taylor (Canterbury Press, 2009)
- *Pilgrimage: a spiritual and cultural journey*, Ian Bradley (Lion 2009)
- *The Pilgrimage to Santiago*, Edward Mullins (Signal 2001)
- *Every Place is Holy Ground*, Sally Welch (SCM 2011)
- *Pilgrimage: a simple guide*, Diocese of Oxford.

Special places of pilgrimage:
The Holy Land, Rome, Santiago de Compostela, Assisi, Lourdes, Taize, Medugorje, Fatima. Iona, Whithorn (Scotland); Croagh Patrick (Ireland); Bardsey island, St David's (Wales); Holy Island, St Cuthbert's Way, Canterbury, Durham, Walsingham (England).
And that only scratches the surface!

INDEX OF FIRST LINES

INDEX OF AUTHORS

INDEX OF SOURCES

ACKNOWLEDGEMENTS

The compiler and publisher gratefully acknowledge permission to reproduce copyright material in this anthology. Every effort has been made to trace copyright holders. If there are any inadvertent omissions we apologize to those concerned; please send information to the publisher who will make a full acknowledgement in future editions.

The Anglican Church in Aotearoa, New Zealand and Polynesia: from *A New Zealand Prayer Book / He Karakia Mihinare o Aotearoa* copyright © The Church of the Province of New Zealand 1989 (p. 42)

Ave Maria Press, Inc., P.O. Box 428, Notre Dame, IN, 46556, www.avemariapress.com: Excerpted and adapted from *Out of the Ordinary* by Joyce Rupp, © 2011. All rights reserved. (p.34)

Fortress Press, admin. Augsburg Fortress Publishers: from *Prayers for Worship Leaders* by Arnold Kenseth and Richard P. Unsworth copyright © 1978. Reproduced by permission. (p.46)

Hymns Ancient & Modern Ltd: from Sally Welch, *Every Place is Holy Ground*, 2011; David Grubb, *Sounding Heaven and Earth*, 2004 (p.23, 29)

Mary Fleeson © Mary Fleeson/www.lindisfarne-scriptorium.co.uk (p.27)

O-books: from *The Celtic Wheel of the Year*, Ropley 2007 (p.16)

Sr. Pauline Derby: from *Pilgrim Prayer* (pp.7, 54)

SPCK: from *The SPCK Book of Christian Prayer*, 2009 (pp. 8, 11, 36, 38, 46, 47) ; David Adam *Tides and Seasons*, 1989 (p.28, 58); David Adam, *The Edge of Glory*, 1985 (p.61)

Wild Goose Resource Group: from Ruth Burges, *Friends and Enemies*, 2004 (p.35); *The Wee Worship Book*, 1999 (p.29)

 Zondervan: from *Book of a Thousand Prayers, The* by Angela Ashwin. Copyright © 1996, 2002 by Angela Ashwin . Used by permission of Zondervan. WWW.ZONDERVAN.COM (p.21)